FEB — 2020

BRIGHT
IDEA
BOOKS

A Toad THAT Explodes

AND OTHER COOL ANIMAL FACTS

by Melissa Abramovitz

Content Consultant

Andrei Alyokhin, PhD
Professor of Applied Entomology
University of Maine

CAPSTONE PRESS
a capstone imprint

Bright Idea Books are published by Capstone Press
1710 Roe Crest Drive, North Mankato, Minnesota 56003
www.mycapstone.com

Library of Congress Cataloging-in-Publication Data
Names: Abramovitz, Melissa, 1954- author.
Title: A toad that explodes and other cool animal facts / by Melissa Abramovitz.
Description: North Mankato, Minnesota : Bright Idea Books, an imprint of Capstone Press, [2019] |
   Series: Mind-blowing science facts | Audience: Age 9-12. | Audience: Grade 4 to 6. | Includes
   bibliographical references and index.
Identifiers: LCCN 2018036890 | ISBN 9781543557725 (hardcover : alk. paper) |
   ISBN 9781543558043 (ebook)
Subjects: LCSH: Animals--Adaptation--Miscellanea--Juvenile literature.
Classification: LCC QH546 .A245 2019 | DDC 591.4--dc23
LC record available at https://lccn.loc.gov/2018036890

Editorial Credits
Editor: Meg Gaertner
Designer: Becky Daum
Production Specialist: Colleen McLaren

Photo Credits
iStockphoto: bschultdesign, 10–11, CampPhoto, 16–17, CraigRJD, 5, Mathisa_s, 8–9,
Moonflash-London, 7, vitranc, 30–31; Science Source: Dr. Morley Read, 20–21, Mark Smith, 25,
Nigel Cattlin, 19, Pascal Goetcheluck, 22–23, Richard Chesher, 14–15; Shutterstock Images: Alen
thien, 13, Ernest Rose, cover (background), Michiel de Wit, cover (foreground), reptiles4all, 27

Printed in the United States of America.
PA48

TABLE OF CONTENTS

AMAZING
Animals

Toads explode. Beetles shoot hot poison. Wasps control spiders' brains. Animals adapt to their environments in amazing ways. These adaptations help them survive.

Cassowaries cannot fly, but they have a powerful kick. They have adapted to living on the ground.

ANIMALS THAT
Explode

More than 1,000 toads exploded in April 2005. They were near a pond in Hamburg, Germany. No one knew why they blew up.

A veterinarian found the answer. Hungry crows had poked a hole in each toad. The toads were alive. Then the crows grabbed the toads' livers. Toads fill with air when they are hurt. But a puffed-up toad with a hole explodes.

Crows eat small animals, insects, nuts, fruit, grains, and dead animals.

Red weaver ants work together to attack an enemy ant.

ANTS EXPLODE

Some ants explode on purpose. They blow up to guard their **colony**. The ant breaks a body part called the **gaster**. The poison inside the gaster explodes. This kills the ant and nearby enemy insects.

Sometimes whales get stranded on the shore. They cannot get back into the ocean.

DEAD WHALES EXPLODE

Dead whales sometimes wash up on beaches. Gas forms as dead bodies **decay**. Gas can make any dead animal explode. But it happens more often in whales. Their thick skin and fat lock gas inside. The body swells up. Boom! Stinky whale parts fly!

DON'T TOUCH!

Sometimes people poke or move dead whales. This can cause an explosion.

CHAPTER 3

READY, AIM,
Fire!

Bombardier beetles have two compartments inside them. Each holds a fluid. The fluids are only dangerous when mixed together. The beetle mixes them when it is afraid. The mixture is a very hot poison. It shoots the poison out of its butt. It can shoot 300 to 700 rounds per second!

12

TAKE YOUR AIM

The beetle can aim the poison it shoots. It aims by moving tiny flaps around the butt.

More than 40 types of bombardier beetles live in the United States.

SEA CUCUMBERS SHOOT BODY PARTS

Sea cucumbers can shoot body parts out of their butts. This scares animals that attack them. Some cucumbers shoot their sticky breathing tubes. The enemy gets tangled inside the tube. Some cucumbers shoot all their body parts. They do not die. They just grow new parts. This usually takes a few weeks.

PEARLFISH

Pearlfish are small, snakelike fish. Sea cucumbers let pearlfish crawl inside their butts. The pearlfish live there. Scientists do not know why sea cucumbers ignore pearlfish.

A pearlfish swims toward the end of a sea cucumber.

Horned lizards use their coloring as camouflage. They blend in with their environment.

HORNED LIZARDS SHOOT BLOOD

Many animals try to eat horned lizards. But horned lizards have a surprise for them. The lizard shoots blood from its eyes. It aims at the enemy's mouth. The blood tastes bad to some animals. This includes coyotes and bobcats. They run away when the blood hits them. Other animals do not mind the taste.

CHAPTER 4

ZOMBIE Animals

Some wasps lay an egg inside a spider. The egg soon becomes a **larva**. The larva drinks the spider's blood. It eats the spider's insides. It also controls the spider's brain. The larva makes the spider spin a strong, special web. The web is perfect for holding a **cocoon**.

The larva kills the spider with poison.
Then the larva spins a cocoon around
itself. The web holds the cocoon.
Soon a new wasp comes out.

The Ichneumonidae are a
family of wasps that lay their
eggs inside other creatures.

FUNGI AND ZOMBIE ANTS

A **fungus** turns carpenter ants into **zombies**. The fungus gets inside an ant. It takes over the ant's brain. It makes the ant leave the ant's colony. The ant climbs onto a leaf above ground. The ant bites the leaf and dies. The fungus forms a stem. The stem pops out of the ant's head. It scatters **spores**. This is so the fungus can spread.

A MIND OF ITS OWN

Fungi have no brains. But they can control ant brains. They started doing this 48 million years ago.

The fungus makes the ant climb a leaf so its spores can spread more easily.

A hairworm exits a dying cricket.

HAIRWORMS AND ZOMBIE CRICKETS

Hairworms live inside crickets. Crickets live on land. They cannot swim. But hairworms must be in water to **breed**. They take over crickets' brains. They force the crickets to find water and jump in. The crickets drown.

The hairworms slither out. They lay eggs in the water. The eggs hatch. A young insect eats a hairworm larva. The young insect grows up. It flies out of the water. A cricket eats the insect. The hairworm larva now grows inside the cricket's body. The cycle begins again.

CHAPTER 5

KILLER
Claws

Pistol shrimp have two claws. The big claw snaps at tasty fish. The quick snap makes water bubbles. The bubbles break. Boom! The noise is louder than a jet engine. The broken bubbles also make a **shock wave**. The powerful shock wave kills the shrimp's prey.

GETTING TOASTY

The shrimp's claw snap also makes heat. The air in the bubbles gets hot. For less than a second, the air gets as hot as the Sun.

Pistol shrimp are also known as snapping shrimp.

ARMED FROGS

Some animals hide their claws. African hairy frogs seem harmless. But they can suddenly sprout blades. When afraid, the frog breaks its own toe bones. Suddenly, sharp claws shoot through its skin!

The tiny nubs at the end of the frog's toes quickly shoot out claws.

GLOSSARY

breed
to produce offspring

cocoon
the silky covering that an insect larva spins around itself

colony
a group of animals of one kind that live together

decay
to break down living matter into its smaller parts

fungus
an organism of a group that produces spores and includes molds, mildews, and mushrooms

gaster
the bulb-shaped body part at the back end of an ant

larva
the stage of an insect's life before it becomes an adult and between the egg and the pupa stages

shock wave
a forceful jolt

spore
a single cell used by fungi, some plants, and other organisms to reproduce

zombie
an animal that is controlled by another creature

TRIVIA

1. Toads eat bombardier beetles. But the beetle can escape from the toad's stomach. The beetle mixes fluids inside itself. The mix explodes. The toad vomits up the beetle. The beetle walks away.

2. Pistol shrimp talk by snapping their claws. A group of snapping shrimp is very loud. The noise blocks sonar. This is a tool ships can use to find objects or other ships. Submarines near snapping shrimp can hide from sonar.

3. Cassowaries cannot fly. But they are the most dangerous birds in the world. They can be 6 feet (1.8 meters) tall. They attack people and animals. They jump and kick. The middle claw on their feet is about 5 inches (13 centimeters) long. It can rip through skin and break bones.

ACTIVITY

ANIMAL ADAPTATIONS

Animals adapt in amazing ways in order to survive. Poison fluids help tiny beetles escape from enemies. Thick fat helps whales stay warm in the ocean. Animals with no survival tools do not last long.

Imagine that you can create a new animal. What is its name? What does it look like? Where does it live? What body parts or abilities help it survive?

First, make a list. Include the animal's name, where it lives, and so on. Figure out what the animal's biggest problem is. Then solve the problem. Does it live in a hot, dry place? Perhaps it needs special skin. How might the skin help it stay cool? Perhaps birds can see it from high in the sky. These birds swoop down to eat it. But birds would not be able to see an animal that changes color. Your animal could blend in with the sand or plants around it.

Then, make a model of your animal. You can use cardboard tubes, egg cartons, modeling clay, and straw. You can use markers, pipe cleaners, and glue. Label the parts of the animal. Explain how these parts help it survive.

FURTHER RESOURCES

Ready to learn more about amazing animals? Check out these resources:

Meister, Cari. *Totally Wacky Facts about Land Animals*. Mind Benders. North Mankato, Minn.: Capstone Press, 2016.

National Geographic Kids: Animals
https://kids.nationalgeographic.com/animals/

Rake, Matthew. *Creatures of the Deep*. Real-life Monsters. Minneapolis, Minn.: Hungry Tomato, 2015.

Want to collect more mind-blowing animal facts? Learn more here!

Amazing Kids Magazine: Amazing Animal Facts!
http://mag.amazing-kids.org/non-fiction/stories/amazing-animal-facts/

Furgang, Kathy. *Animal Records: The Biggest, Fastest, Grossest, Tiniest, Slowest, and Smelliest Creatures on the Planet*. National Geographic Kids. Washington, D.C.: National Geographic, 2015.

INDEX